Art Profiles
For Kids

PAUL CÉZANNE

Mitchell Lane
PUBLISHERS

P.O. Box 196
Hockessin, Delaware 19707
Visit us on the web: www.mitchelllane.com
Comments? email us: mitchelllane@mitchelllane.com

ART PROFILES FOR KIDS

Titles in the Series

Art Profiles
For Kids

PAUL CÉZANNE

Kathleen Tracy

Mitchell Lane
PUBLISHERS

P.O. Box 196
Hockessin, Delaware 19707
Visit us on the web: www.mitchelllane.com
Comments? email us: mitchelllane@mitchelllane.com

Printing   1   2   3   4   5   6   7   8   9

Library of Congress Cataloging-in-Publication Data
Tracy, Kathleen.
  Paul Cézanne / by Kathleen Tracy.
      p. cm.—(Art profiles for kids)
  Includes bibliographical references and index.
  ISBN 978-1-58415-565-2 (library bound)
  1. Cézanne, Paul, 1839–1906—Juvenile literature. 2. Painters—France—Biography—Juvenile literature. 1. Title.
ND553.C33T73 2007
759.4—dc22   20.95
[B]
                                                                         2007013176

ABOUT THE AUTHOR: Kathleen Tracy has been a journalist for over twenty years. Her writing has been featured in magazines including *The Toronto Star's Star Week*, *A&E Biography* magazine, *KidScreen* and *Variety*. She is also the author of numerous biographies and other nonfiction books, including *Mariano Guadalupe Vallejo*, *William Hewlett: Pioneer of the Computer Age*, *The Watergate Scandal*, *The Life and Times of Cicero*, *Mariah Carey*, *Kelly Clarkson*, and *The Plymouth Colony: The Pilgrims Settle in New England* for Mitchell Lane Publishers. She divides her time between homes in Studio City and Palm Springs, California.

ABOUT THE COVER: The images on the cover are paintings by the various artists in this series.

PHOTO CREDITS: p. 20—Getty images; pp. 8, 30—paintings by Edouard Manet; all other artwork by Paul Cézanne.

PLB

3 9082 11090 9838

Table of Contents

Art Profiles for Kids

Cézanne painted *Self Portrait on a Rose Background* around 1875, a year after he first exhibited paintings with the Impressionists. The critical response to his work was brutal, with reviewers making fun of his use of colors. His personal life was equally stressful. Fearful his father would cut off financial support, he kept his girlfriend and their child a secret—even though Cézanne was a thirty-six-year-old man.

CHAPTER 1
one

Betrayal

If you walk through any comprehensive art museum, hall after hall will be devoted to the Impressionists. Their names are now a who's who of art—Monet, Manet, Pissarro, Renoir, Cézanne. Many of their works are considered masterpieces; palettes that influenced generations of artists that followed, from Vincent van Gogh to Pablo Picasso.

But in the mid-1880s, the Impressionists were considered a bad artistic joke. From the moment they had dared to challenge traditional styles, French art critics had ridiculed their efforts, and the top Parisian galleries refused to show their canvases. Because they were determined to continue exploring new ways of using colors, some of these original Impressionists were forced to truly live as starving artists for many years. Claude Monet was frequently supported financially by friends and spent several years scraping by while living in a small country village with his mistress and their child while perfecting his style. Paul Cézanne lived off a skimpy allowance from his tightfisted father, and the only paintings he sold were to a local grocer who accepted them as payment for food.

The last thing any of these artists needed was more bad press.

In 1886, famed novelist and former art critic Émile Zola announced the next book in his Rougon-Macquart series of novels, which depicted life in contemporary France under the rule of Emperor Napoléon III. It would be set in the world of the Impressionists. After the announcement, most of the painters were worried—except for Paul Cézanne. Zola had been his friend since childhood and had been an early advocate of the Impressionist

Manet's painting of Emile Zola, detail

movement. And Zola had used his friends for writing ideas before—a fictionalized character based on Cézanne, named Claude Lantier, had already made a brief appearance in one of Zola's previous books, *The Belly of Paris*.

Even before the story was published as a newspaper serial, Cézanne knew that Zola planned to make Lantier the protagonist of his new novel, which was named *L'Oeuvre* (*The Work*). Part of him might have even been a bit flattered. But Cézanne was in for a shattering surprise when Zola sent him a finished copy of the book in April 1886.

The depiction of Claude Lantier in *L'Oeuvre* was a brutal, unflattering portrait of a sullen artist wracked by torturous self-doubt—a man painfully unsure of himself around women and pathologically insecure about his talent. Lantier's best friend is a writer named Pierre Sandoz who has achieved great success, and it is through his eyes that Lantier's downfall is seen.

From the start, Zola admitted the book be roman à clef in nature, telling an agent, "It's my whole youth, I've put myself and all my friends in it."[1]

The early portion of the novel recounts the characters' childhood friendship and early years as struggling aspiring artists in Paris. Not only did Zola use his own real-life experiences, he also incorporated many intimate details from Cézanne's life, including his having an affair that led to the birth of his first child. Then he added harsh fictional elements, such as Lantier's boorish and cruel treatment of his mistress as she grows older and no longer resembles the youth in his paintings.

Lantier is also depicted as a distant father. When the character's emotionally neglected twelve-year-old son dies, at first Claude grieves, but then slowly begins to see the lifeless body through an artist's eyes.

He tried to resist it at first, but the attraction grew stronger and stronger to the point of obsession, until at last he gave way, fetched out a small canvas and set to work on a study of the dead child. For the first few moments his vision was fogged by tears. . . . Work soon dried his eyes and steadied his hand, and the dead body of his son became simply a model, a strange, absorbing subject for the artist. . . . The waxlike texture of the skin, the eyes like holes wide open on the void, everything about it excited him . . . he stood back to see the effect; he was pleased, and a vague smile appeared on his lips as he worked.

When Christine looked up she found him completely absorbed and, as she burst into tears again, all she could find to say was:

"Oh, you can paint him now. He'll keep still enough this time!"[2]

The final third of the book describes the painter's descent into a kind of madness. His perceived inability to create the masterwork that will be his legacy drives him to despair. He ends up hanging himself in front of his uncompleted picture, and the writer burns the painting that symbolizes Lantier's failure.

The controversial novel generated intense buzz throughout Paris' artistic communities. Monet and most of the other Impressionists were appalled. They feared that the book would give critics of their movement additional ammunition to belittle their work. "In essence," Auguste Renoir said angrily, "he has used his talent to profit from the destruction of other people's reputations."[3]

Cézanne's response was more complicated. Some associates reported that the painter enjoyed the chapters that recounted the characters' childhoods and youthful adventures.[4]

In *Pour Moi, Cézanne,* a "fictional autobiography" based on Cézanne's letters, author Earl Mayan describes the artist's sense of betrayal. Having already been warned of *L'Oeuvre*'s content by fellow painter Renoir, Cézanne opens Zola's novel with a premonition of dread. "I instinctively believed that the moment I had feared for many years was at hand and the final wedge was about to be driven between us: that this particular package contained the confirmation of my old friend's break with his past associations; and I was thinking of this in a personal sense."[5]

His fears were confirmed. "Ignorance ran through *L'Oeuvre*, a repetitious and sometimes malicious distortion of fact. . . . To Zola, it was clear to me . . . controversy was more important than the truth."[6]

Although the public may not have initially known on whom Claude Lantier's character was based, Cézanne lamented, "my friends in the radical group, and my enemies at the Académie would quickly recognize the story as a reflection of my life. . . .

"It hurt terribly that Zola saw me only as a misfit, as an eccentric, a buffoon, a man totally alienated from a society that respected practical accomplishment over everything else. The fabrication he had created of our lives became even worse as he camouflaged it in the name of aesthetic idealism; I wept openly when I read the passages which damned the radical movement: he had, by humiliating us publicly, demeaned the lifetime of struggle we had put into our art."[7]

Yet Cézanne never directly confronted Zola. In her article for *The New Yorker*, Rachel Cohen said, "Immediately after receiving his copy of *L'Oeuvre*, Cézanne wrote Zola a polite note in which he thanked 'the author of the Rougon-Macquart for this good testimony of remembering' and asked 'permission to allow me to shake his hand, in memory of years gone by.' Then there was an incontestable absence. After this note, Zola and Cézanne neither wrote nor spoke to each other again."[8]

In truth, *L'Oeuvre* cut too close to the bone. Cézanne was beset by sometimes crippling self-doubt, and the Impressionist movement did appear to be floundering after the death of its inspirational leader Édouard Manet in 1883. But while a fascinating insight into the minds and creative passions of the Impressionists, in the end, Zola's book was not prophetic. Cézanne may not have ever been completely satisfied with his work, but he proved to be a man ahead of his time. In the years following his death, Paul Cézanne would become known as the father of modern art, finally earning the recognition that had eluded him in life. But the road to immortality would be full of obstacles and detours.

The Second Empire

Zola's series, the Rougon-Macquart, was an ambitious twenty-book project set during the rule of Emperor Napoléon III. It follows the lives of two very different branches of a family: the wealthy Rougons, who possess a seemingly insatiable appetite for money and power, and the down-to-earth Macquarts, who struggle to overcome various personal failings and obstacles, such as alcoholism and emotional frailty.

While on one level the books are pure melodrama filled with all the lust, intrigue, and deception of any good soap opera, Zola also used the stories to showcase the social injustices and questionable politics of the times, reflecting the country's unrest with the rule of their emperor.

During the nineteenth century, the French government underwent several dramatic overhauls. The Revolution of 1789 ended the reign of the Bourbon monarchy, and in 1799 Napoléon Bonaparte was named First Consul. Five years later Bonaparte crowned himself emperor. After Napoléon's defeat at Waterloo in 1815, the French monarchy was restored with Louis XVIII. In 1824 Louis was overthrown by Charles X. In 1830, Louis-Philippe was named king and ruled for the next eighteen years.

The working and middle classes once again revolted, and Charles-Louis-Napoléon Bonaparte was elected president in 1848. Legally limited to one term, Bonaparte and his followers overthrew the government in 1851. He named himself Emperor Napoléon III and the Second Empire was born.

Political corruption was rampant—the emperor either deported or executed his enemies—and the middle class grew wealthy at the expense of the working classes. Interestingly, though, Napoléon III oversaw many socially liberal changes, such as granting greater freedom of the press. He also approved the expansion of the county's railroad system, improving the infrastructure of Paris through massive public works programs, and undertaking the construction of the Suez Canal in Panama.

The emperor's ambitions would ultimately be his downfall. He declared war against Prussia, which proved disastrous and marked the beginning of the German Empire. After he was captured at the Battle of Sedan in 1870, he was exiled to England. Louis-Napoléon died on January 9, 1873. He was France's last monarch.

Napoléon III

Bread and Eggs (1865) was painted during Cézanne's Dark Period, the years in Paris between 1861 and 1870. Cézanne's depression about his lack of critical recognition was reflected in his use of dark colors and frequent use of black.

two

Blood Brothers

Nestled in the southeast corner of France between the Mediterranean Sea and the Italian Alps, the spectacular natural beauty of Provence has drawn visitors to the region since Roman times. The warm, dry climate is reminiscent of Southern California—as is the lifestyle. Unlike the urban bustle of Paris, life in Provence moves at a slower pace—so slow that many young people growing up in its quaint villages dreamed of leaving for the big city. Paul Cézanne would be no exception.

On January 19, 1839, Paul Cézanne was born in the ancient city of Aix-en-Provence (ayks-ahn-proh-VAHNS), which sits on the Arc River. His father, Louis-Auguste, who was already forty years old, made his living manufacturing felt hats. His mother, Anne-Élisabeth-Honorine Aubert, was Louis' much-younger girlfriend who for a while had worked in his shop. Two years after Paul, the couple had another child, Marie.

Although it's not uncommon now for an unmarried couple to have a child, in the nineteenth century it was considered socially shameful. Such children were often referred to as bastards and were treated as being inferior in some way to someone born to married parents. Even though Louis and Anne eventually married in 1844, Paul would struggle his entire life with the sense he was an unaccepted outsider; feelings that possibly stemmed back to his being born illegitimate.

Although he is described as being an agreeable child, he was also prone to sudden, inappropriate temper tantrums that were shocking to witness. Then just as suddenly they would pass. In public, Paul was so shy

The Artist's Father, painted between 1865 and 1866. Cézanne used a palette knife instead of a brush to paint the picture. Cézanne depicts his father reading *L'Evénement,* a newspaper that frequently published Zola's articles. He also reproduces one of his still life paintings on the wall behind his father.

and timid that his younger sister, Marie, took on the role of his protector.

In grade school Cézanne's best friend was a sweet-natured boy named Philippe Solari, who would later become a sculptor. After school, the two boys would explore Aix or play in any of the many fountains the city was famous for. In those days, herds-men still drove cattle through town on the way to the market, filling the streets with the smell of livestock.

At home, Paul enjoyed a close relationship with his mother, but Louis was not a family man. "He loved [Mother] dearly," Marie once wrote about her brother, "and was no doubt less afraid of her than of our father, who was not a tyrant but was unable to understand anyone except persons who worked in order to get rich."[1]

And indeed, Louis-Auguste Cézanne was ambitious. In 1848 he opened the Cézanne and Cabassol Bank with his partner, Joseph Cabassol. Suddenly, the former merchant was one of Aix's most prominent citizens.

After having attended the local public school, Paul enrolled at Saint-Joseph, a Catholic boarding school, when he was eleven. Two years later, he entered Bourbon College. Paul was an excellent student, and his father naturally assumed his son would pursue some prestigious career, such as law. It just showed how little he knew about his son.

While at Bourbon, Paul met a fellow outcast named Émile Zola. Born in Paris, Zola's family had moved to Aix when he was a toddler. His father, François, was an engineer who hoped to strike it rich by building a dam. He died before the project could be completed, leaving his wife, Émilie, with a mountain of debt and only a meager pension on which to support their son. Soon, however, she was befriended by a local politician, who pulled strings to get Émile accepted at Bourbon College.

At first it seemed as if Zola's stay at the school would be grim. Between his lisp, Italian heritage, and coming from a poor family, Émile was constantly taunted by the other students, who all came from wealthy or important families. Years later, Zola recalled his misery in *La Confession de Claude,* saying his classmates "were pitiless, soulless, like all children. I must be a strange creature, capable only of loving and weeping, for I looked for affection, I suffered, from the very first steps I took. My years at school were years of tears. I had in me the pride of loving natures. I was not loved, for I was not known, and I refused to let myself be known."[2]

Zola's school life turned around the day Cézanne rescued him from being pummeled by bullies in the school courtyard. The two boys quickly became friends and, along with Baptistin Baille, were known as *les trios inseparables*—the three inseparables.

In *L'Oeuvre,* Zola remembered their times together, swimming in the local river, with a near-romantic fondness. "They practically lived in the water and the combination of pure water and sunshine seemed to prolong their childhood, so that even when they were already young men they still sounded like a trio of laughing urchins as they ambled back . . . after a day on the river."[3]

The bond between Zola and Cézanne was especially strong. They shared a dream of finding success in the arts—Paul as a painter, Émile as a writer—"a soaring ambition and a passionate devotion to the life of the spirit. . . . The two boys escaped on holidays for long days of wandering over the mountains, mutually exciting each other by their common dream of artistic glory,"[4] Zola writes.

Paul was a diligent student who did well in English but, ironically, poorly in art classes. Zola, on the other hand, won awards for his painting and drawing skills. He would spend hours daydreaming about living the bohemian life of a writer, free from the grind of an office job, and being his own boss. Cézanne got caught up in Émile's fantasy, which further inflamed his yearning to make his dream of being a painter come true. Louis, however, expected his son to get a law degree then work at the family bank, and Paul was afraid to tell his father what he really wanted to do with his life. For a long time he kept his passion for art a secret.

Finally, inspired by Zola's constant encouragement, Paul enrolled in some drawing classes at a local art school, École Gratuite de Dessin, which is now the Granet Museum. His teacher was the museum's director, Joseph Gibert. Under his direction, Cézanne drew using both live models and classical sculptures. Even so, art remained a pastime, and Cézanne continued to dutifully attend the college to prepare for a life as a banker.

In 1858, Zola left Aix to move to Paris with his mother. Rather than drift away from Paul, the separation made them even closer. As Rachel Cohen wrote in *The New Yorker:*

> The young writer and the aspiring painter kept up a passionate correspondence. Cézanne, a fine Latinist, sent long, humorous poems in complicated metres. Zola's eyes were already turned toward artistic success, and he often placed his talents second to his friend's. "Give me a great painter, or I shall never forgive you," he exhorted. And, protectively, "I don't want anyone to spoil my Cézanne for me."[5]

Without Zola around to initiate outings or to read with, Cézanne became depressed and morose. "Since you left Aix, I've been weighed down by a deep melancholy," he told Émile in one of his letters.[6]

The classical themes of rape, murder, and kidnapping are represented in Cézanne's *The Abduction,* from 1867. Just who is being abducted has been debated. Some believe it is supposed to be Hercules carrying off Alcestis after saving her from the underworld, but most scholars agree it depicts Hades, the Greek god of the underworld, and Persephone.

Even in his teens, Cézanne already suffered from the mood swings that would later characterize his emotional instability as an adult. According to biographer Meyer Schapiro, in letters written during that time, "He appears in these documents an unsociable, moody, passionate youth who is given to compulsive acts which are followed by fits of despair. He is one of those ardent temperaments tormented by profound feelings of inadequacy. . . . His youthful letters alternate between ironical self-disparagement and fulsome verses on the joys of nature and imaginary loves."[7]

In 1859, Louis bought a mansion called Jas de Bouffan, which became the new family home. His wealth didn't impress Paul, nor did it make him want to take a job at the bank. That was okay with Louis—if Paul didn't want to follow in the family business, he could become a lawyer.

Cézanne dutifully obeyed but also got his father's permission to keep taking drawing classes. Even though Louis wanted his son to have a respectable career, he also had no problem with him pursuing his "hobby."

Through it all, Zola would write Cézanne fiery letters, urging his friend to follow his dream. Finally, Paul told his father he wanted to be a painter and admitted he had no desire to be a lawyer or a banker. Louis was understandably shocked, but he was more concerned than angry. Having grown up poor, he wanted his son to have a secure job. Paul's mother supported his passion for painting, as did Marie. For almost a year the family debated the issue, with Louis hoping that with time, Paul would reconsider.

Even though Cézanne continued to press his father, Zola's impression was that Paul was actually hesitant to move away from the comforts of home. Cézanne hated the idea of supporting himself, but because Zola dropped out of school, he was convinced to follow suit. He took a clerical job at the docks to make just enough money to survive but hated going to an office. He soon quit and spent all his time writing. He was so poor there were times he supposedly was forced to catch sparrows on his windowsill for his next meal. If Zola was willing to sacrifice so much for his art, Cézanne felt he needed to be equally committed.

Even so, he had no desire to starve. He finally managed to convince his father that he would never know whether he could make a living at painting unless he were allowed to study it properly. In turn, Louis decided that perhaps the best way to get painting out of his son's system would be to let him see what life as a struggling painter would be like. He gave Paul his blessing—and a small allowance—to move to Paris.

Louis, along with Marie, accompanied Paul on his trip and stayed in Paris for several weeks before returning to Aix. Reunited with Zola, Cézanne looked forward to starting a new life in the City of Lights and meeting others who shared his passion for painting.

Being an untrained, unknown artist in Paris would be more depressing and demoralizing than Cézanne could have ever imagined.

Aix-en-Provence

The history of Cézanne's hometown goes back over two thousand years. Aix was one of the first colonies established by the Romans after they conquered Gaul, the area of Western Europe that in ancient times included modern France, Italy, and Belgium, as well as parts of Switzerland and Germany.

Founded in 123 BCE by a Roman consul, or governor, named Sextius Calvinus, Aix was an important city because it lay along trade routes leading to the Rhône Valley. It also was a strategic military post because any invading tribe from Gaul could be stopped at Aix before it reached Italy. Beyond its geographical attributes, Aix attracted Romans who came to enjoy the natural hot springs that ran beneath the city.

After the Roman Empire declined, Aix and the surrounding countryside fell into centuries of turmoil, with one tribe after another conquering and plundering the region. Finally, during the Middle Ages, a wall with thirty-nine towers was built to protect the city. Thus secured from attack, Aix grew into a cultural and artistic center of Provence and was named the provincial capital.

The French Revolution (1789–1799) changed all that. The new government stripped the city of its title as provincial capital and handed that honor to the port town of Marseille to the south. As Marseille thrived, Aix withered. Although still home to several universities and the region's legal courts, the population dwindled and Aix became little more than a market town with few opportunities for success. For more than a century, Aix languished.

After World War II, the city was reborn. Between 1930 and 1959, the population more than doubled. Aix's cultural and artistic history, combined with the region's stunning natural beauty, made it a popular tourist destination. It is also a respected learning center and the home of three universities: Université de Provence; Université de la Méditerranée, and the Université Paul Cézanne.

Although its appeal has also brought increased traffic congestion and overly crowded cafés, Aix remains one of France's most vibrant cities and an important link to the country's past.

Cézanne's home in Aix-en-Provence

By 1875, Cézanne, along with other artists such as Monet, was known as an Impressionist. The term was coined by art critic Louis Leroy, who had made fun of their then-unorthodox style after the group's first exhibit in Paris a year earlier.

Self-Doubt

At Zola's urging, Cézanne enrolled at the Académie Suisse, an art studio run by painter Charles Suisse. Cézanne spent every morning at the studio, then browsed museums and galleries in the afternoon or visited Aix artist Joseph-François Villevielle (vee-uh-vee-ELL), who was now living in Paris.

For as much as he wanted to be happy, Cézanne was miserable. He found Paris cold, cramped, and dirty compared to the bright open spaces of Provence. He was a country boy completely out of place. Zola, on the other hand, loved the city and, except for the fact that he was dirt poor, enjoyed his life there. It upset Cézanne to think that he and Zola had grown apart. Émile the outcast and awkward daydreamer had turned into Zola the ambitious aspiring writer and sophisticated young man.

After the initial excitement of being reunited in Paris wore off, Cézanne began to see less and less of Zola, pining for their former life together. Lonely and depressed, he was consumed by homesickness.

"I must admit I am none too cheerful," he wrote to a friend back in Aix. "I fritter my life away in every direction. . . . I thought that by leaving Aix I should leave behind the boredom that dogged me there. In fact, all I have done is change my address and the boredom has followed. I have left behind my parents, my friends, and some habits, that's the whole difference."[1]

After just a month in Paris, Cézanne started talking about giving up painting and going home to Aix. It seemed Louis had known his son better than Paul cared to admit. Zola, of course, was appalled. He wrote, "To

Cézanne painted *Young Girl at the Piano—Overture to Tannhauser* in 1868. The girl is his sister, the woman his mother. Some art critics feel the mood of this painting is more peaceful than others from his Dark Period—most likely because he was in Aix rather than in Paris.

have fought for three years to make this trip and then to throw it away like a straw. . . . Age has developed his [Cézanne's] obstinacy, without giving him a rational basis on which to be obstinate. . . . He won't even discuss what he is thinking; he has a horror of argument . . . because he may have to change his mind if his adversary is proved right."[2]

It didn't help Cézanne's mood that he was often teased at the art studio for his "provincial," or country, ways—the way he dressed, the way he talked . . . even the way he drew. He was also extremely opinionated and sullen, which made him even more of an outcast.

The irony is it was all a cover. Cézanne wanted nothing more than to be accepted by his peers and share in their camaraderie. So he immersed himself in painting—and in this he was an outsider. At the time, painting was taught with very strict rules regarding composition. Paul thought all the rules prevented artists from fully expressing themselves—since everyone saw the world through their own unique eyes, how could one style possibly allow for the artist's vision to come across? By adhering to rules about use of color and light, everyone's work "felt" a whole lot like everyone else's.

Rather than encourage such free thinking, Villevielle suggested Paul just conform and keep his opinions to himself. This depressed Cézanne even more.

One day Zola stopped by Paul's rooms and saw his suitcases packed. Rather than try to talk him out of leaving, Émile reminded Cézanne he had promised to paint his portrait. Paul agreed to stay in Paris to work on it. In a fit of frustration, he destroyed the canvas when he couldn't get it just the way he wanted. Zola, who had always been Cézanne's biggest supporter, now had second thoughts. "Paul may have the genius of a great painter but he'll never have the genius to become one," he wrote. "The least obstacle makes him despair."[3]

To Cézanne, it was simply a matter of not settling for less. He had come to Paris with the dream of being a great painter, but he had done nothing to stand out from all the other hopefuls. The thought of being considered mediocre was unacceptable—better to give up painting completely than to be reminded every day of his failure. He returned to Aix and told Louis he was ready to be a banker.

After two weeks he changed his mind and yearned to return to Paris.

While part of him wanted to be in Aix where he was comfortable and cared for, part of him needed to be in Paris trying to develop his talent. Because of these conflicting desires, wherever Cézanne was, he longed to be elsewhere. Rather than choose one over the other, Paul would end up traveling back and forth between the two cities for much of his life. This dual existence would influence the development of his artist's eye.

Louis had come to accept with surprising calm that Paul would never take over the family business. But if Louis were going to invest in Paul's future, he wanted some kind of tangible return for his money. He insisted that if his son pursued art, he should dedicate himself to it completely.

Victor Chocquet was such a strong supporter of the Impressionists that some accused him of being mildly insane. He commissioned both Renoir and Cézanne to paint portraits of him and his wife. Renoir showed the collector as confident and distinguished. In Cézanne's painting (left), Victor's downcast expression seems to reflect the artist's own malaise.

Cézanne left for Paris in November 1862, better prepared to face the challenges ahead. Things were also looking up for Zola. Through a family friend he got a job at Hachette, one of the largest publishers in Paris. Even though he only worked in the mail room, just being around the book world inspired him. The dependable paycheck allowed him to buy some clothes and eat regularly. At night he worked on his writing. He eventually gave the firm's founder, Louis Hachette, some of his poetry. The publisher suggested Zola try his hand at prose and asked him to submit a short story to one of the company's children's magazines. He also doubled Zola's salary, which allowed him to rent a nicer apartment big enough for him and his mother.

His previous anger at Cézanne for going home was forgotten, and Zola once again acted as Paul's personal guide. Every Thursday, Zola would invite Cézanne and others to his apartment, mostly to talk about

Throughout his life, Cézanne was inspired by the natural beauty of Provence in general and Jas de Bouffan in particular. *The Pond* was painted at the family home in 1876, and is an example of painting en plein air—outside and capturing natural light on the canvas.

art. Other times he would take Paul to the studios of other painters he had gotten to know, such as Claude Monet and Edgar Degas—young men who, like Cézanne, were more interested in expressing themselves than adhering to the classical style.

"The concept of modernity—the notion that art has to advance constantly . . . independent of the past—was well established," notes author Meyer Schapiro. "To become a painter then was to take a stand among contending schools and to anticipate an original personal style. It was, above all, to be an individual."[4]

Their attitudes were in part a reaction against Romanticism, an artistic movement that evolved around 1800 and remained popular for the next fifty years. Romanticism wasn't characterized by a particular style but by a painting's emotional, sometimes melodramatic, content. Often the scene portrayed was religious in nature, so Romanticism came to be associated with conservative attitudes.

Realists considered themselves the anti-Romantics. They presented subjects as they look in real life, rather than an artist's interpretation of them. It was no coincidence the movement followed the rise of photography, which captured moments of real life with unsparing clarity.

The Realist movement was spearheaded by Frenchman Gustave Courbet, who believed that it was an artist's responsibility to pursue and depict truth, whether it was the harsh working and living conditions of the lower classes or highly erotic images. He was more concerned with presenting an accurate portrayal and less mindful of keeping the lines of his colors perfectly matched.

Realism soon became equated to loose morals and irresponsible youth—much the way rock and roll was when it evolved in the late 1950s. The young Cézanne was hardly a wild, sex-love-rock-n-roll kind of guy in his personal life, nor did his work reflect the gritty social realism of Courbet's. But when it came to his instincts about following painting traditions, he was a revolutionary, so he felt a kinship with the Realists.

"Cézanne . . . had come to Paris just after the battle over Realism, a turning point in art," notes Schapiro. "From the very first, he declared himself a Realist, although in practice his art hardly conformed to the Realist approach. As a young man in conflict with his strict bourgeois [upper class] father and restless from unsatisfied dreams of love, he was attracted by the advanced artistic milieu [social setting] in Paris with its freer life and rebelliousness against authority . . . the assertion that direct experience was superior to imagination."[5]

As usual, the majority of the people in power, in this case the art academics who advanced the traditional schools that taught artists how to paint, did not like having their authority challenged. The young artists were largely ignored—until they publicly challenged the status quo in 1863.

L'École des Beaux-Arts

In the nineteenth century, the top art school in France was L'École des Beaux-Arts. Located in Paris near the Louvre museum, it was founded in 1648 as a government-run school that taught everything from architecture and drawing to engraving and gem cutting. Louis XIV selected its top graduates to paint portraits of members of his family or to decorate royal palaces and apartments. In 1863, Napoléon III made the school independent, and it was renamed École des Beaux-Arts.

The school was divided into the two specialties: painting and sculpture, and architecture. Both courses concentrated on teaching classical art such as Greek and Roman sculpture and the work of the Renaissance masters such as Leonardo da Vinci and Raphael.

The architecture program attracted students from all over the world. American graduates of the school would go on to design many famous buildings, including the Boston Public Library, Boston Museum of Fine Arts, New York's Grand Central Station, and the Metropolitan Museum of Art.

The painting curriculum was rigid. All students had to study drawing in a very specific order—first engravings then plaster casts and finally using live nude models. Only after they mastered those skills were they allowed to begin painting.

Attending L'École des Beaux-Arts was an important step in becoming a professional artist. Aspiring artists prepared for the extremely difficult entrance exam by studying with established artists, or masters. After they finished working at the studios, or ateliers, students would fill the local cafés to discuss and debate art.

L'École des Beaux-Arts

"They literally lived, breathed, and drank art—twenty-four seven," reports art historian Natasha Wallace. "The cafés were but informal extensions of the ateliers and the École, and the Masters would hold court at a table of their followers to argue and discuss theories and technique and . . . critique art. It would be at the cafés that the vanguard of art flourished and from which the Impressionists came."[6]

Today the school has an enrollment of around 500 students and is known for its extensive collection of classical art.

Cézanne used workers at Jas de Bouffan as his models for his three different versions of *The Card Players*, with one, two, and three players respectively. The small brushstrokes he used were a direct influence from Impressionism. The muted colors, along with his depiction of the players as being completely absorbed in their game, adds an unexpected emotional depth to the series.

four

The Impressionists

The most important annual event of the art world was the Paris Salon, a public art show that could make an artist's career. Cézanne and the others all submitted their work. Most members of the selection jury were conservative academics who were loathe to promote independent thinking, so they promptly rejected the paintings.

Again, just as the 1960s were a time of radical change in American pop culture, with performers like Elvis and the Beatles challenging mainstream musical tastes, in the 1860s this group of young rebellious painters would begin an artistic revolution. Rather than accept the Salon's decision, they protested, angrily denouncing the narrow-minded academics. The controversy got so heated that Emperor Napoléon III became involved, worried that the situation could escalate into a political hot potato. His solution was to establish the Salon des Refusés, a secondary showing of works not accepted into the main Salon.

Naturally, the public flooded to the Salon des Refusés to see what the fight was all about. The young artists' work was exposed to a large audience for the first time. Édouard Manet's controversial *Déjeuner sur l'Herbe* (*Luncheon on the Grass*) was both the hit and the scandal of the exhibition. Looking at the painting now, it hardly seems scandalous—two clothed men are relaxing on the ground while one female companion, who is nude, sits beside them; the other appears to be picking something up off the ground. The painting was revolutionary. Instead of smoothly blending the paint, his brushstrokes are clearly visible. Even the woman's

Manet's *Luncheon on the Grass* was considered scandalous when it was first exhibited in 1863, but for free-thinking young artists of the time, it was a courageous display of independence. The clothed men represent Manet's younger brother and their brother-in-law.

nude body is realistically flawed. The original jury labeled the painting obscene because it showed a nude woman in a contemporary setting.

Cézanne was deeply influenced by Manet's work. "The motive of the picture haunted him throughout his life," wrote author Roger Fry, "and he never gave up the hope of realizing a great design, conceived in a similar spirit."[1]

Over the next four years, Paul traveled back and forth between Paris, where he immersed himself in study, and Aix, where he would apply his new skills to both portraits and still-life paintings. Slowly he was developing a unique style, characterized by his use of strong colors and his instinctive use of proportion, the relative size of objects on a canvas.

Despite his growing maturity as an artist, Cézanne was still a social disaster. He longed to be one of the gang who gathered at the Café Guerbois to discuss art. Instead, his critical opinions of others, defensiveness about his own work, and general lack of social skills deterred friendships. The others might have respected his talent, but few sought out his company. Nor did he have any better luck with women, by whom he felt rejected. Considering this, maybe it's not surprising that much of Cézanne's work during his early years are filled with morbid images, such as kidnapping, rape, and murder, in works titled *The Autopsy, The Murder,* and *The Abduction,* with heavy, almost violent brushstrokes. Feeling rejected as an artist and as a man left Cézanne increasingly bitter.

Nor was Paul any happier when painting. Moody and impatient, he would fly into irrational rages if models didn't sit perfectly still, complaining that the work was now forever ruined. He was equally hard on himself, destroying countless canvases he felt were inferior.

Year after year he submitted work to the Paris Salon. Year after year it was turned down. In 1866, his frustration boiled over and he wrote an indignant letter:

I cannot accept the unfair judgment of colleagues whom I myself have not commissioned to appraise me. . . . I wish to appeal to the public and show my pictures in spite of their being rejected. My desire does not seem to me extravagant, and if you were to ask all the painters in my position, they would reply without exception that they disown the jury and that they wish to take part in one way or another in an exhibition which should be open as a matter of course to every serious worker. Therefore, let the Salon des Refusés be re-established.[2]

His request was turned down.

Zola took up the artists' cause. Having published his first novel in 1865, *Confession de Claude,* which he dedicated to Cézanne, Zola left Hachette the following year and was working as a book reviewer for a daily newspaper named *L'Evénement*. He wrote many articles for other publications, passionately defending Manet and the other Realists. Zola empathized with their desire to break free from convention and experiment with new forms of expression. He managed to anger so many conservatives and traditionalists that by 1868, no mainstream French newspapers would buy his articles.

While Zola made a name for himself as a champion of the avant-garde, Cézanne continued experimenting with different styles and motifs. The dark colors, violent content, and heavy paint strokes of his earlier works gradually gave way to lighter compositions—both in color and theme.

Perhaps part of the change can be attributed to having finally found a female companion. In 1869, at age thirty, he met nineteen-year-old Hortense Fiquet. All that's known about her early life is that she was the daughter of a bank teller, and her mother died shortly before she met Paul.

Up to meeting Hortense, Paul had avoided women whenever possible, telling Zola, "I don't need them." But he also admitted he had always "been afraid to even try to find out what they were good for."[3]

It's speculated that the artist may have felt pressured to start a relationship with someone, anyone, because Zola was about to be married. Cézanne may have feared—irrationally—that he would lose Émile's friendship; that Zola would devote himself to his new wife and forget about Paul.

Hortense became Cézanne's mistress and his primary model, but oddly, Paul insisted on keeping their relationship a secret from his father—although his mother and sisters knew. Even after she gave birth to their son three years later, he refused to acknowledge her or his child, fearful his father would be angry and cut him off financially.

When France unexpectedly declared war on Prussia in 1870, Cézanne had no intention of joining the army. He defied a government order that all able-bodied men report for duty. He left Paris with Hortense and hid out in L'Estaque, a quaint fishing village twenty miles from Aix.

Pyramid of Skulls, is an example of Vanitas Art, a genre of still life that depicts macabre objects—in this case human skulls. By 1901, Cézanne had moved beyond Impressionism and the first hints of Cubism became evident.

The vivid colors and strong light of the Mediterranean coast would have a profound effect on Cézanne. Years earlier he had told Zola that he preferred working en plein air, or in natural light, as opposed to painting inside a studio. But it wasn't until after the end of the Franco-Prussian War that Cézanne followed through on that desire, prompted by his time in L'Estaque. He packed up Hortense and the baby and went to study under Camille Pissarro, another radical.

"He was more than a teacher and friend to Cézanne; he was a second father," says biographer Meyer Schapiro. "Pissarro taught Cézanne a method of slow, patient painting directly from nature. . . . [This approach] thus made painting for Cézanne more purely visual. . . . His first flower pieces date from this time."[4]

What truly set Pissarro, Manet, Monet, and the others apart from traditionalists was their use of color and light. Instead of mixing blue and yellow paint to make green, they put yellow paint next to blue paint. When the viewer looked at the canvas, their brain would still "see" green, or the impression of green. The overall sense, or essence, of the painting was more important than the details of it. Also, the use of black paint was avoided. Finally, up to then everything, even landscapes, was painted inside studios. By working outside, en plein air, Pissarro showed Cézanne how to capture the effects of sunlight.

After the request for another Salon des Refusés was turned down in 1872, the artists decided to put on their own show. In April of 1874, a group of thirty painters, including Monet, Renoir, Pissarro, Cézanne, and Degas, presented an exhibition of their work at a Parisian studio owned by a photographer. One critic who attended, Louis Leroy, was particularly unimpressed and made fun of the then-unorthodox style. Mocking the title of Monet's *Impression: Sunrise,* he wrote: "Impression—I was certain of it. I was just telling myself that, since I was impressed, there had to be some impression in it . . . and what freedom, what ease of workmanship! Wallpaper in its embryonic state is more finished than that seascape."[5]

After that review, Pissarro and the others became known as the Impressionists.

Despite Leroy's assessment, the public was intrigued. Over the next dozen years the Impressionists would hold eight more exhibits. Interestingly, the group's spiritual leader, Édouard Manet, never participated. Instead, he continued to submit to the Salon, believing that only by breaking through there would the Impressionists really achieve lasting success.

In fact, despite their exhibitions and the gradual acceptance of their style, the Impressionists still struggled to find financial success. By the time they did, in the late 1880s, Impressionism had become an accepted form and was no longer considered cutting edge. It would be many years before its importance as an art form would be fully appreciated.

For his part, Cézanne would drift away from the Impressionists. He would take the lessons learned and use them to develop a unique style that finally brought him the respect and recognition he had so desperately craved.

Franco-Prussian War

The stretch of flat land in northern Europe below the Baltic Sea has played an important part in European history. In ancient times, the area was inhabited by Baltic tribes in the east and Slavic tribes in the west. In the seventh century, a German tribe known as Prussians settled there and gave the land its name.

Over the next several centuries, invaders came and went, and Prussia changed hands numerous times. It finally became its own sovereign state, the Kingdom of Prussia, in 1701, and quickly prospered. By 1772, led by King Frederick II, Prussia included parts of modern-day eastern Germany, northern Poland, and some of Russia.

Prussia eventually became the most dominant German state. When German Prince Leopold was nominated to the vacant Spanish throne in 1870, French leaders became nervous that Prussia and Spain might join forces to attack France. Although Leopold's name was withdrawn from consideration under strong diplomatic pressure, German Chancellor Otto von Bismarck saw French paranoia as a perfect opportunity to unite the German states into one empire. He sent a telegram to French officials that made it seem as if Prussian King William I were still considering putting a member of his royal family on the Spanish throne.

The ploy worked, and on July 19, 1870, Napoléon III declared war— but the emperor's military advisers had greatly underestimated the strength and organization of the Prussian army. A month later, on August 31, Napoléon was captured at the battle of Sedan. A new French government was installed, but within weeks, Paris was under siege. It finally surrendered on January 28, 1871. The Treaty of Frankfurt gave Germany the French state of Alsace and half of neighboring Lorraine—a provision that infuriated the French. In addition, France had to pay Germany 5 billion francs. As Bismarck dreamed, King William I was named emperor, and Germany was on its way to being Europe's most powerful country. The ill will between France and Germany would fester for the next forty-five years and would ultimately lead to World War I.

Frederick the Great

Large Bathers is one of three paintings of bathers Cézanne worked on between 1899 and 1906. Throughout his career, Cézanne struggled to depict the human form to his satisfaction. He left many canvases partially finished and even destroyed others because of it. It is also why many of his paintings ultimately focus on color and feeling rather than accurate portrayal of form.

five

The Father of Modern Art

By 1880, Cézanne had already started moving away from the short brushstrokes that characterized Impressionism in favor of thicker, parallel strokes. This gave his compositions more texture, mass, and depth. *The Gulf of Marseille Seen from L'Estaque* is a good example of the effect. This period is sometimes called his "constructive" phase.

Although he fully embraced the Impressionist belief that one could find true art only by painting directly from nature, he differed in that he also believed paintings needed structure. He once commented that his goal was to turn Impressionism into "something solid and durable, like the art of the museums."[1] This innovation would be the inspiration for many Post-Impressionist painters, including Paul Gauguin and Vincent van Gogh.

But in 1886, after reading *L'Oeuvre*, Cézanne's future looked bleak. Not only would the book expose all his self-doubts and paranoia, his father would find out about Hortense and their son. It left Paul with no choice but to finally tell the truth—after seventeen years of lies.

Louis was understandably hurt. And once the secret was out, Paul's mother and sister, Marie, a devout Catholic who greatly disapproved of her brother's living "in sin," pushed him to get married. Cézanne obliged, and on April 28, 1886, he and Hortense were married in Aix. Six months later, Louis died.

In many way, Paul's estrangement from Émile Zola was the greater loss. Losing the man who had been his closest friend and only confidante for the past thirty-four years left a yawning void in Paul—there was nobody else who understood him the way Zola had. He felt completely alone.

Louis Cézanne's death made Paul a wealthy man, giving him the freedom to come and go as he pleased. Although he loved his son a great deal, his relationship with Hortense was one of convenience, not passion. Whenever Paul traveled back to Aix, she stayed in Paris with their son. Cézanne had as few friends in Provence as he did in Paris. Other than his mother and sisters, he rarely saw anyone. He drifted away from Pissarro and spent more and more time alone in reclusive isolation.

"He became violently anti-social," biographer Lawrence Hanson wrote. "Suspicion, latent in him all his life, was allowed full rein; it poisoned every relationship. With every year his detestation of his fellow men seemed to grow and his efforts to appear even passably civil dwindled to next to nothing. He criticized everything and almost everybody; only his son . . . escaped his scathing tongue."[2]

The only thing he seemed to value was his painting. Ironically, as Cézanne the man deteriorated into a horridly unlikable human being, Cézanne the painter channeled all his energies and devotion to painting. By losing everything, he was able to find his artistic vision.

"The painter possesses two things: an eye and a brain," he explained. "The two must work together. Both must be developed. But developed to meet the needs of the painter: the eye by looking at nature, the brain by logically organizing the sensations which lead to the form of expression."[3]

In other words, an artist needed to use his intellect as much as his creativity to give paintings form.

"Lines parallel to the horizons give breadth . . . lines perpendicular to this horizon give depth," he said. "For us men, nature is more depth than surface so we must introduce into our light vibrations, represented by reds and yellows, enough bluishness to convey the feeling of air."[4]

Inspired by this epiphany, Cézanne worked obsessively, making Aix his permanent base. He concentrated on a handful of subjects: apples, landscapes, the nearby Mont Sainte-Victoire, and studies of bathers. He

In the last days of his life, Cézanne used his longtime gardener, Vallier, as his subject. The artist's style is noticeably different now than earlier in his career; most notably the use of longer, parallel brushstrokes that gave more texture and depth. These works are considered Post-Impressionist and form the basis for modern art as we have come to know it.

would return to the same subject over and over, each time looking at it from a slightly different vantage point.

Cézanne dropped so far out of sight that as the years passed he was forgotten by all but a few of his former colleagues. The public at large had never known who he was. He might have died in obscurity had it not been for a shrewd art dealer named Ambroise Vollard, who arrived in Paris in 1887 when he was twenty-nine years old.

Vollard heard about Cézanne from some artist friends and tracked him down in 1895. One can only imagine Cézanne's surprise when the young dealer bought 150 canvases. Vollard was taking a huge risk—Cézanne himself was virtually unknown and his work had not been shown in Paris for over twenty years.

Apple, a Bottle and a Milk Pot shows Cézanne's deviation from Impressionism. Rather than using the "impression" method of colors side by side, he blended colors so that his objects have more depth and seem more three-dimensional than works of Monet, Renoir, and the others.

The exhibition was a success. It cemented Vollard's reputation as one of Paris' most important dealers and gave Cézanne the creative recognition that had alluded him his entire life.

Vollard continued to promote and sell Cézanne's work. The more people who saw the paintings, the more his reputation grew as a great innovator. Young painters began traveling to Aix to see Cézanne and pick his brain. The outcast was suddenly the master.

"An artist must study his subject, get a firm sense of it, and find a way to express himself forcefully and with distinction," he wrote to Émile Bernard in 1904. "Taste is the best judge, but it is rare. Art is accessible to only a very small number of people. The artist must shun opinions not based on the intelligent observations of essentials. He must avoid thinking like a writer, which so often distracts the painter from his true goal—the direct study of nature."[5]

Recognition mellowed Cézanne somewhat, and he became less reclusive. But having no one with whom to share his success—specifically, without Zola—it must have seemed hollow. While Cézanne had spent the time since *L'Oeuvre* shunning people and the spotlight, Zola had become an even more famous writer. His criticism of Alfred Dreyfus' conviction for spying led the French government to charge Zola with "defamation." When convicted, he fled to England, where he lived in exile for a year. Shortly after his return to France, he was found dead from carbon monoxide poisoning, the result of a blocked chimney.

When news of Zola's death reached Cézanne, the old painter locked himself in his studio and howled in grief. Four years later, in 1906, Aix dedicated a statue to Zola. Cézanne was seen standing off to the side, weeping.

Although his health had started to fade, Cézanne still painted every day. Two years after his mother's death in 1897, the family home, Jas de Bouffan, had been sold, so he built a studio on the outskirts of Aix. He walked there each day from his apartment in the city.

In a display of temper, Cézanne refused to hire a carriage one day after the rates went up. On the way home, he was caught in a rainstorm. He caught a cold, developed pneumonia, and died a week later, on October 22, 1906.

His work and innovation live on. His experiments with geometric forms laid the foundation for Cubism, made most famous by Pablo Picasso, and later, Abstract art. His influence on these forms is why many consider him the Father of Modern Art.

"Cézanne's art has a unique quality of ripeness and continuous growth," comments art historian Meyer Schapiro. "He admitted to the canvas a great span of perception and mood, greater than that of his Impressionist friends. . . . He paints with a virile brush solidly, or in the most delicate sparse watercolor, and is equally sure in both. . . . He can be passionate and cool, grave and light; he is always honest.

"Cézanne's work not only gives us the joy of beautiful painting; it appeals too as an example of heroism in art. For he reached perfection, it is well known, in a long and painful struggle with himself."[6]

There's an old saying that great art only comes from great pain. If that's true, then indeed Cézanne will be remembered as one of the greatest artists who ever lived.

J'Accuse!

Alfred Dreyfus

In 1894, papers discovered in the office of a German military attaché led French authorities to believe a spy was selling secret to the Germans. The man who was ultimately accused was Captain Alfred Dreyfus, who indeed had access to the information but adamantly voiced his innocence. In a secret court-martial, Dreyfus was convicted, stripped of his military rank, and sentenced to life imprisonment on Devil's Island, a hellish penal colony located off the coast of South America.

Because Dreyfus was Jewish, his conviction ratcheted up the anti-Semitism that was already rampant in France. Political right-wingers pointed to the Dreyfus Affair, as it was known, as proof that the government was seriously flawed. Newspapers openly attacked Jews, claiming Dreyfus was just another example of how Jews could not be trusted.

Then a strange thing happened. Lieutenant Colonel Georges Picquart, who was openly anti-Semitic, discovered evidence that Dreyfus may have been wrongly convicted. His investigation led him to identify Major Walsin Esterhazy as the spy. To Picquart's dismay, the army did not want to hear it and promptly shipped him off to Tunisia so that he could not pursue the matter. A military court ignored the evidence he had gathered and acquitted Esterhazy.

Despite the obvious cover-up, few in the military, or the public, were willing to defend a Jew. But Émile Zola was. Outraged by the army's conduct, he wrote a scathing article that began, *"J'accuse!"* (I accuse you!), claiming the military was guilty of an illegal conspiracy. The government promptly charged Zola with libel. He was found guilty.

He avoided jail by moving to England. A year later, his was granted amnesty and returned to France, where the furor over Dreyfus was still raging.

Dreyfus was given a new trial in 1899 and was again convicted, but his sentence was reduced to ten years. In September, French President Émile Loubet pardoned Dreyfus. In 1906 Dreyfus was cleared of blame and his rank was restored.

Zola never lived to see it. Although unconfirmed, years later a man confessed on his deathbed that he had murdered the writer by intentionally blocking his chimney. He had been angry over Zola's support of Dreyfus.

CHAPTER NOTES

Chapter 1. Betrayal

1. Rachel Cohen, "Artists's Model," *The New Yorker,* November 7, 2005, http://www.accessmylibrary.com/coms2/summary_0286-12600355_ITM

2. Émile Zola, *The Masterpiece,* translated by Thomas Walton (Oxford, England: Oxford University Press, 1993), pp. 308–309.

3. Earl Mayan, *Pour moi, Cézanne,* http://home.earthlink.net/~klavir/Cézanne_intro.html

4. Cohen.

5. Mayan.

6. Ibid.

7. Ibid.

8. Cohen.

Chapter 2. Blood Brothers

1. Philip Callow, *Lost Earth: A Life of Cézanne* (Chicago: Ivan R. Dee, 1995), p. 20.

2. F.W. Hemmings, *Émile Zola* (Oxford: Clarendon Press, 1953), p. 7.

3. Callow, p. 31.

4. Roger Fry, *Cézanne: A Study of His Development.* (New York: Macmillan, 1927), p. 5.

5. Rachel Cohen, "Artists's Model," *The New Yorker,* November 7, 2005, http://www.accessmylibrary.com/coms2/summary_0286-12600355_ITM

6. Lawrence Hanson, *Mortal Victory: A Biography of Paul Cézanne* (New York: Holt, Rinehart and Winston, 1959), p. 19.

7. Meyer Schapiro, *Paul Cézanne* (New York: Harry N. Abrams, 1962), p. 22.

Chapter 3. Self-Doubt

1. Lawrence Hanson, *Mortal Victory: A Biography of Paul Cézanne* (New York: Holt, Rinehart and Winston, 1959), p. 35.

2. Philip Callow, *Lost Earth: A Life of Cézanne* (Chicago: Ivan R. Dee, 1995), pp. 66–67.

3. Hanson, p. 42.

4. Meyer Schapiro, *Paul Cézanne* (New York: Harry N. Abrams, 1962), p. 24.

5. Ibid.

6. John Singer Sargent Virtual Gallery, *École des Beaux-Arts,* http://jssgallery.org/Essay/Ecole_des_Beaux-Arts/Ecole_des_Beaux-Arts.htm

Chapter 4. The Impressionists

1. Roger Fry, *Cézanne: A Study of His Development* (New York: Macmillan, 1927), p. 8.

2. John Rewald, *The History of Impressionism* (New York: Museum of Modern Art, 1961), p. 142.

3. Lawrence Hanson, *Mortal Victory: A Biography of Paul Cézanne* (New York: Holt, Rinehart and Winston, 1959), p. 95.

4. Meyer Schapiro, *Paul Cézanne* (New York: Harry N. Abrams, 1962), p. 26.

5. Louis Leroy, "L'exposition des impressionnistes," *Charivari,* April 25, 1874, pp. 2–3.

Chapter 5. The Father of Modern Art

1. "New Cézanne," *Time,* March 29, 1954, http://www.time.com/time/magazine/article/0,9171,819695,00.html

2. Lawrence Hanson, *Mortal Victory: A Biography of Paul Cézanne* (New York: Holt, Rinehart and Winston, 1959), p. 180.

3. Ibid., p. 182.

4. Ibid., pp. 182–183.

5. Michael Doran, editor. *Conversations with Cézanne* (Berkeley: University of California Press, 2001), p. 30.

6. Meyer Schapiro, "Modern Art," http://www.artchive.com/artchive/C/Cézanne.html

1839	Paul Cézanne is born on January 19 in Aix-en-Provence, France.
1844	His father, Louis-Auguste Cézanne, marries his mother, Anne-Elisabeth-Honorine Aubert. Paul enters school.
1848	Louis-Auguste opens Aix's only bank.
1850	Paul goes to Saint-Joseph boarding school.
1852	Paul attends Bourbon College and becomes friends with Émile Zola.
1859	Family moves to Jas de Bouffan, an estate in Aix. Paul begins studying law.
1861	Paul moves to Paris to study at Académie Suisse; returns home.
1862	He briefly takes a job at father's bank, then goes back to Paris to study at École des Beaux-Arts, but he is not accepted. He begins "dark" or "romantic" period.
1869	Paul meets Hortense Fiquet.
1870	During the Franco-Prussian War, he and Hortense stay in L'Estaque near Marseille.
1872	Son, Paul, is born. Cézanne works with Pissarro in Pontoise.
1873	He enters Impressionist Period.
1874	His work is exhibited with other Impressionist paintings. The exhibit is poorly received.
1877	Cézanne sends paintings to the third Impressionist exhibition, where again they are poorly reviewed.
1880	He enters "constructive" period.
1882	After years of rejection, his portrait of his father is accepted by the Salon. It is the only time the Salon accepted his work during his entire career.
1886	After the publication of Zola's *L'Oeuvre*, he ends friendship with Zola; he marries Hortense in April; father dies in October.
1895	Ambroise Vollard exhibits 150 of Cézanne's paintings, which greatly boosts the artist's popularity.
1897	His mother dies.
1899	He sells Jas de Bouffan and moves to final residence at 23 Rue de Boulegon.
1902	He builds Chemin des Lauves studio.
1904	Galleries in Paris and Berlin exhibit his paintings.
1906	Cézanne dies of pneumonia on October 22.

TIMELINE

1809	First blackboard is used in a classroom.
1825	Telegraph inventor Samuel Morse helps establish National Academy of Design.
1826	Joseph Niepce creates the first photograph.
1834	Wheaton College is established.
1844	Civil War photographer Mathew Brady opens New York studio.
1848	Gold is discovered in California.
1867	Vassar College becomes the first woman university to offer an art history class.
1870	Massachusetts makes art a mandatory course in state schools.
1871	P.T. Barnum starts his circus.
1888	Ballpoint pens are patented, but they don't become popular until 1945.
1891	Thomas Edison invents the first movie camera.
1905	First nickelodeon opens in Pittsburgh, Pennsylvania.
1917	The first jazz record, "Livery Stable Blues," is released.
1928	Walt Disney's *Steamboat Willie,* the first sound-synchronized cartoon, is released.
1929	Museum of Modern Art opens in New York.
1931	Elementary school teacher Ruth Shaw develops fingerpaints.
1940	Prehistoric drawings are discovered on cave walls in Lascaux, France.
1943	Architect Frank Lloyd Wright begins working on the Guggenheim Museum.
1946	*Highlights* magazine debuts.
1964	*Time* magazine coins the term *op art,* or *optical art,* which uses lines or patterns to show movement or illusions.

FURTHER READING

Books

Burleigh, Robert. *Paul Cézanne: A Painter's Journey.* New York: Abrams Books, 2006.

Harris, Nathanial. *Paul Cézanne* (Artists in Their Time). London: Franklin Watts, 2003.

Venezia, Mike. *Paul Cézanne* (Getting to Know the World's Greatest Artists). Danbury, CT: Childrens Press, 1998.

Wenzel, Angela. *Paul Cézanne: How He Amazed the World* (Adventures in Art). London: Prestel Publishing, 2005.

Works Consulted

Callow, Philip. *Lost Earth: A Life of Cézanne.* Chicago: Ivan R. Dee. 1995.

Cohen, Rachel. "Artists's Model." *The New Yorker.* November 7, 2005. http://www.accessmylibrary.com/coms2/ summary_0286-12600355_ITM

Doran, Michael. *Conversations with Cézanne* (Documents of Twentieth-Century Art). Berkeley: University of California Press, 2001.

Fry, Roger. *Cézanne: A Study of His Development.* New York: Macmillan, 1927.

Hanson, Lawrence. *Mortal Victory: A Biography of Paul Cézanne.* New York: Holt, Rinehart and Winston, 1959.

Hemmings, F.W. *Émile Zola.* Oxford: Clarendon Press, 1953.

John Singer Sargent Virtual Gallery. École des Beaux-Arts. http://jssgallery.org/Essay/ Ecole_des_Beaux-Arts/Ecole_des_Beaux-Arts.htm

Lallemand, Henri. *Cézanne: Visions of a Great Painter.* New York: Todtri Productions Limited, 1994.

Leroy, Louis. "L'exposition des impressionnistes." *Charivari, April 25,* 1874.

Mayan, Earl. *Pour moi, Cézanne.* http://home.earthlink.net/~klavir/Cézanne_intro.html

"New Cézanne," *Time,* March 29, 1954, http://www.time.com/time/magazine/ article/0,9171,819695,00.html

Rewald, John. *The History of Impressionism.* New York: Museum of Modern Art, 1961.

Schapiro, Meyer. "Modern Art" (excerpt). http://www.artchive.com/artchive/C/ Cézanne.html

———. *Paul Cézanne.* New York: Harry N. Abrams, 1962.

Zola, Émile. *The Masterpiece.* Thomas Walton, translator. Oxford, England: Oxford University Press, 1993.

Zupnick, I. L. "The Social Conflict of the Impressionists. Zola's Opinions versus Evidence in Portraits." *College Art Journal,* Vol. 19, No. 2 (Winter, 1959–1960).

On the Internet

Artchive.com, *Paul Cézanne* http://www.artchive.com/artchive/C/Cézanne.html

Impressionism—Biography of Paul Cézanne http://www.impressionniste.net/ Cézanne_paul.htm

GLOSSARY

advocate (AD-voh-ket)
A supporter.

avant-garde (AH-vont GARD)
Art, whether literature, painting or music, that is new or experimental or ahead of its time.

bohemian (boh-HEE-mee-in)
Unconventional; artsy.

bourgeois (bourzh-WAH)
Having to do with members of the middle class of a country.

composition (kom-poh-ZIH-shun)
The combination of elements in a painting and how they are put together visually.

contemporary (kun-TEM-puh-rayr-ee)
Happening at the same time; happening during one's lifetime.

embryonic (em-bree-AH-nik)
In an early stage of development.

epiphany (ee-PIH-fuh-nee)
Moment of clear understanding.

erotic (eh-RAH-tik)
Relating to sexual desire.

landscape
A depiction of nature or the outdoors.

libel (LY-bul)
False statements printed about someone.

motif (moh-TEEF)
The theme or subject of a painting.

palette (PAL-et)
A handheld tray on which an artist mixes paints; it also can refer to the grouping of colors in a painting.

prophetic (prah-FEH-tik)
Predicting the future.

prose (PROHZ)
Any writing that is not poetry.

roman à clef (roh-MAH-nah-KLAY)
A type of novel in which real people and events are thinly disguised and depicted as fictional.

status quo (STAH-tus KWOH)
The existing, accepted conditions or way of doing things.

still life
A painting of inanimate objects.

INDEX